Tricks with Dollar Bills

BY ROBERT MANDELBERG

Sterling Publishing Co., Inc.
New York

Library of Congress Cataloging-in-Publication Data

Mandelberg, Robert.
    Tricks with dollar bills : another way to make your money
disappear / Robert Mandelberg.
        p. cm.
    Includes index.
    ISBN-13: 978-1-4027-3856-2
    ISBN-10: 1-4027-3856-0
    1. Tricks. 2. Paper money. 3. Dollar, American. I. Title.

GV1559.M26 2006
793.8—dc22

                                2006005131

2 4 6 8 10 9 7 5 3 1

Published by Sterling Publishing Co., Inc.
387 Park Avenue South, New York, NY 10016
© 2006 by Robert Mandelberg

Illustrations by Bob Steimle

Distributed in Canada by Sterling Publishing
c/o Canadian Manda Group, 165 Dufferin Street
Toronto, Ontario, Canada M6K 3H6
Distributed in the United Kingdom by GMC Distribution Services
Castle Place, 166 High Street, Lewes, East Sussex, England BN7 1XU
Distributed in Australia by Capricorn Link (Australia) Pty. Ltd.
P.O. Box 704, Windsor, NSW 2756, Australia

Printed in China
All rights reserved

Sterling ISBN-13: 978-1-4027-3856-2
            ISBN-10: 1-4027-3856-0

For information about custom editions, special sales, premium and
corporate purchases, please contact Sterling Special Sales
Department at 800-805-5489 or specialsales@sterlingpub.com.

Contents

Introduction

So you have a few dollars in your pocket. What are you going to do with them? Oh, sure, you can go out and spend them on a donut and a cup of coffee, but what fun would that be? The donut will only add extra calories and the coffee will keep you up all night. Why not read through this book and see how you can have some *real* fun with dollar bills? In the following pages, you will learn a wide range of tricks and challenges with dollars. I will also provide quirky phenomena and fascinating facts about greenbacks that you can use to stump, baffle, and entertain your closest friends and your parole officer. Clever sleight-of-hand maneuvers, fascinating mind-reading tricks, and amazing stunts await you. So skip the donut and dig into this book to see how you can generate better interest on your dollars.

$leight of Hand

"Now you see it, now you don't." . . . How many times have you heard that insufferable line? Well, the good news is that the next time you hear those words, they will be coming from *your* lips. After reading this chapter, you'll be so good at making money disappear, people will think you're running for office! Although these tricks are very effective and a lot of fun to perform, they do require practice. Spending a few minutes a day to perfect the moves will guarantee a flawless performance every time. And once you learn the techniques, feel free to alter them to suit your own style. Read on and see how you can double your money, or turn one dollar into five dollars, or even find a hundred dollar bill in a piece of fruit.

DISAPPEARING DOLLARS

Invite a subject to sit in a chair in the center of the room. You will have a small stack of dollar bills within arm's distance. As you stand in front of your subject, take one bill from the stack and crumple it into a ball. With a few quick hand motions, you are able to make the bill disappear into thin air. Take another dollar, perform the same movements, and it, too, vanishes. Repeat the maneuver until the stack is depleted. What makes this trick so entertaining is that everyone in the audience will see how it is done. Everyone, that is, except the subject!

The secret: Stand directly in front of your seated subject, holding a crumpled dollar bill in your hand. Tell him to keep his eye on the dollar, as you lift the hand with the dollar bill slightly above his head and then bring it back down, keeping the dollar in plain sight. Repeat this motion three times. The third time you lift your hand up, simply release the dollar bill and gently toss it over the subject's head. It will be above his eye level, so he won't see it being released—but the audience will! Then quickly rub your hands together and show the spectator the dollar has disappeared. When the trick is over, the audience will be hysterically laughing, the subject will be completely confused, and there will be a sea of crumpled dollars on the floor behind him.

FRENCH DROP

This is clearly one of the all-time best sleight-of-hand maneuvers ever invented. Begin by folding a dollar bill four times until it is a small, convenient square. With your palm facing up, grip the bill with your thumb and forefinger—I prefer using my left hand (fig. 1). As you will note, your thumb and forefinger are in a semicircle.

With your right hand (palm facing down), slide your thumb into the semicircle. Keep your other four fingers on your right hand straight and flat (fig. 2).

Now pretend to grab the bill with your right hand. This will be done in a two-step process. First, bring the four straight fingers of your right hand downward so that you are hiding the dollar bill from the view of your audience (fig. 3).

As you do this, simply drop the bill from the thumb and forefinger of your left hand and let it fall into your palm. Remember, the fingers of your right hand are blocking the audience's view, so no one will see you dropping the bill (fig. 4).

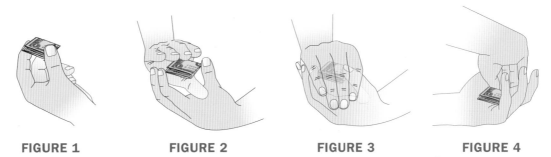

FIGURE 1 **FIGURE 2** **FIGURE 3** **FIGURE 4**

Now close your right hand completely—as if you've just snatched the bill. This is the most crucial part of the trick. You have to perform two moves simultaneously. Move #1: Swing your closed right hand in front of you (fig. 5). All eyes will be on your right hand, since that is where they think the dollar bill is. It helps if you look at your right hand as well. Move #2: Your job is to slowly and nonchalantly turn your left hand over and grip the dollar bill in your pinky and ring finger. Important: Do NOT close your left hand in a fist and snatch it away. If you do, it will be obvious that you're hiding something in your hand.

This trick is easiest to do while you and your audience are seated around a table. While the spectators are looking at your right (empty) hand, bring your left hand to the edge of the table (fig. 6). Drop the bill on your lap and then rest your left hand on the table palm down (fig. 7).

A simple way to end this trick is to simply open your right hand and show that the dollar has disappeared (fig. 8). Of course, the audience will insist on you opening your left hand—which is why you drop the bill in your lap. For more creative endings and tricks using the French Drop, see the next two entries.

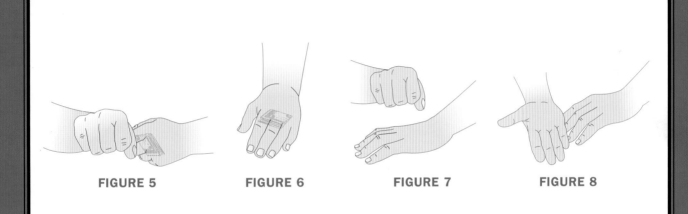

FIGURE 5   **FIGURE 6**   **FIGURE 7**   **FIGURE 8**

11

FRENCH SWITCH

Here is a chance for you to use your magic for financial gain. In French Switch, you will be able to mysteriously change a one dollar bill into a five dollar bill (or a twenty or a hundred if you like). By using the French Drop technique (explained on pages 8–11), you will be able to execute the switch quite effectively. But like the French Drop, this requires some practice to perfect. Here are the moves:

Before beginning the trick, fold a five dollar bill (or a twenty or a hundred) four times and hide it securely under the pinky and ring finger of your right hand (fig. 1). Once you have the bill in place, you then break into the French Drop. Start by folding the one dollar bill four times. Then hold it between the thumb and index finger of your left hand, forming a semicircle with your palm up (fig. 2). The next step requires a slight variation from the French Drop. When you slide your right thumb into the semicircle of your left hand, you must keep your right pinky and ring finger bent, so that the five dollar bill remains hidden (fig. 3). Next, bring your right index finger and middle finger down to block the audience's view of the one dollar bill. While its view is obscured, drop the one dollar bill into your left palm (fig. 4).

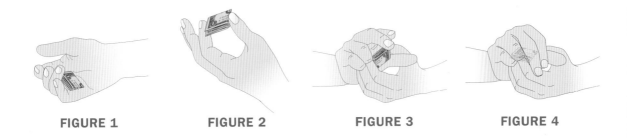

FIGURE 1   **FIGURE 2**   **FIGURE 3**   **FIGURE 4**

You're almost home free, hang in there! At this point, the one dollar bill is in your left hand and the five dollar bill is in your right hand. Your job now is to get rid of the one dollar bill. Here's how: Close your right hand, pretending that you just snatched the one dollar bill. Move your closed right hand in front of you (fig. 5). Stare at your right hand and tell the audience that you have just executed a miracle. As your audience is transfixed on your right hand, casually bring your left hand to your lap and drop the one dollar bill (fig. 6). When that is completed, slowly bring your left hand on the table, as if it has been there all along. Now, all you have to do is present the finale. Open your right hand and reveal the bill (fig. 7). Unfold it to show the audience how you've mysteriously transformed a one dollar bill into a five (fig. 8).

FIGURE 5

FIGURE 6

FIGURE 7

FIGURE 8

SWEET MAGIC

Sweet Magic is a great trick to use as a follow-up to the French Drop (see page 8). Before starting the trick, borrow a one dollar bill from your spectator and ask him to initial it in pencil. Then fold the dollar bill four times and follow steps 1 through 5 of the French Drop. When you have completed the drop into your palm and revealed your empty right hand to the audience, you will have the folded bill hidden in your left hand. Maneuver the bill so that it rests under the middle finger of your left hand, hidden from your audience (fig. 1).

Ask a spectator to hand you a sugar packet—or any artificial sweetener, as long as it comes in a small packet. Take the packet in your left hand and hold it firmly between your thumb and index finger (fig. 2). With one quick motion, rip open the bottom of the sugar packet (fig. 3). As the sugar falls from the packet, release the folded dollar bill and let it fall to the table (fig. 4). It will look as though it fell out of the packet. When your spectator accuses you of having a different dollar hidden in the sugar packet, you can convince him otherwise by unfolding it and showing him his initials (fig. 5).

FIGURE 1   **FIGURE 2**   **FIGURE 3**   **FIGURE 4**   **FIGURE 5**

HIDDEN FIVER

Here is another opportunity for you to turn one dollar into five dollars. All you will need is a one dollar bill, a five dollar bill, a handkerchief, and some nerve. Out of view of the audience, start by taking a five dollar bill and folding it four times (fig. 1). Then take a crisp one dollar bill and hold it in both hands between your thumb and index fingers, with the front of the bill facing the audience (fig. 2). Make sure to keep your other fingers open so that the audience can see there is nothing hidden under them.

The folded five dollar bill will be hidden behind the one dollar bill by the bottom left corner, held in place by your left thumb (fig. 3). You can gesture with your right hand as you speak, so everyone sees that nothing is hidden in it. Now you're going to fold the one dollar bill in half lengthwise, sandwiching the five dollar bill inside the fold. Hold the one dollar bill with your right thumb and index finger on the outside of the dollar bill, keeping the hidden five dollar bill secure in the fold (fig. 4).

FIGURE 1

FIGURE 2

FIGURE 3

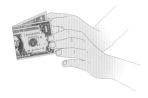
FIGURE 4

You can now gesture with your left hand, showing the audience that nothing is hidden in it. Next, fold the one dollar bill again lengthwise, and as you do, transfer it to your left hand and casually squeeze the hidden five a little lower so it hangs below the edge of the one dollar bill (fig. 5). Notice how you're now using your left hand to block the audience's view. Fold the one dollar bill in half from top to bottom and hold it up in your left hand between your thumb and index finger. The five dollar bill is hanging out of the one dollar bill slightly—but don't worry, your left hand is still blocking the audience's view (fig. 6).

Ask a member of the audience to pick up the handkerchief from the table and inspect it. Once she sees that nothing is hidden in the handkerchief, she hands it to you. Place the handkerchief over the one dollar bill. After chanting your favorite magical phrase, use your right hand to snatch away the handkerchief *and* the one dollar bill in one smooth motion (fig. 7). Make sure to pinch the five dollar bill in your left thumb and index finger. As the handkerchief is pulled away, all that will remain is the five dollar bill. Unfold the bill for the audience. Magically, you have transformed a one dollar bill into a five right before their eyes (fig. 8)!

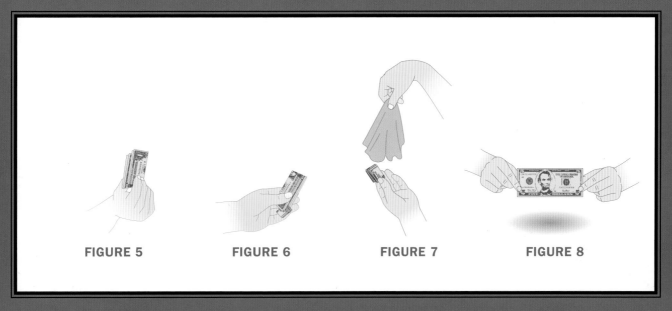

FIGURE 5 FIGURE 6 FIGURE 7 FIGURE 8

21

BILL IN FRUIT

What you are about to read is a fun version of a world-class trick used extensively by professional magicians. It requires more effort than the other tricks in this book, but it is well worth it. You will magically make a dollar bill disappear and then reappear inside an orange.

Begin by asking a spectator for a bill (the larger the better, but a one dollar bill will work just fine). Ask the spectator to initial the bill with a pencil (fig. 1). Then roll up the bill *tightly* (fig. 2). Next, hold the rolled-up bill in your hand and cover it with a handkerchief (fig. 3). Ask another spectator to feel the handkerchief from the outside to confirm that the dollar bill is inside (fig. 4). Then have the spectator pass the handkerchief around so the other observers can feel that the bill is still there (from the outside).

While the spectators are inspecting the handkerchief, pull out three oranges from a bag and place them on the table. When the handkerchief has made its way through the audience and back to you, take it and place it in your jacket pocket. Then ask an audience member to select one of the three oranges on the table.

FIGURE 1   FIGURE 2   FIGURE 3   FIGURE 4

Once her selection is made, reach inside your jacket looking for the handkerchief. After searching for a few moments, announce to your audience that the handkerchief has disappeared along with the rolled-up dollar. Then ask an observer to peel the orange that was selected. In the center of the orange, there will be a rolled-up dollar bill. And not just any dollar bill—the original bill that your spectator initialed!

Here's how: Before you begin, you will need to bore a small hole in an orange. This can be easily accomplished by working a pencil into the orange (figs. 5 and 6). Then place the orange in a bag along with two other oranges. You will also need to roll up a dollar bill and place a piece of scotch tape around it to make sure it stays rolled up (fig. 7). Then hide it under the handkerchief. You can then tape the bill to the handkerchief to keep it in place (fig. 8). This is the dollar your spectators will be feeling in a moment. You are now ready to begin.

Ask a spectator to take a dollar bill out of his wallet and initial it. When he hands it to you, roll it up and place it in your left hand. Drape the handkerchief over your left hand to cover the dollar bill. Now hold the initialed bill in your palm so it will be hidden when you remove the handkerchief.

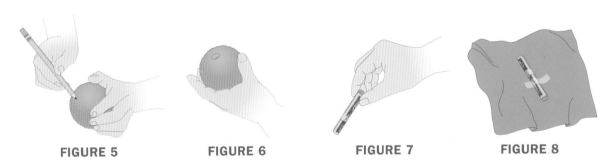

FIGURE 5 **FIGURE 6** **FIGURE 7** **FIGURE 8**

Pull the handkerchief away with your right hand, grabbing it by the preset dollar (fig. 9). In your left palm you will be concealing the bill that was initialed. Give the handkerchief to the audience for verification. As the spectators are busy inspecting it, reach into your bag for an orange. In one smooth motion, insert the dollar bill into the hole you created (fig. 10). Then pull out each orange and place it on the table.

Next, take the handkerchief with the preset bill and place it in your jacket pocket. Now it's time to "force" the right orange. Start by asking a spectator to select one. If the correct one is selected, put the other two back in the bag. If a wrong orange is selected, place it in the bag, hold the remaining two in your hands and ask another spectator to select one. If the correct one is selected, place it on the table, while placing the third orange in the bag. If the wrong one is selected again, place it in the bag, leaving the correct one to be placed on the table.

After pretending to search for the handkerchief in your jacket, give the selected orange to a spectator and ask her to peel it. She will soon reach the rolled-up bill. (fig. 11). And when she unrolls it, she discovers it's the same bill that was initialed earlier (fig. 12).

FIGURE 9

FIGURE 10

FIGURE 11

FIGURE 12

DOUBLE DOLLARS

Here is another chance to use your magic for profitable gain. In Double Dollars, you will turn one dollar bill into two. Start by borrowing a dollar bill from a spectator. Show your audience that there is nothing in your hands except for the dollar bill. Fold the dollar in half and begin rubbing it on your elbow. Then rub your hands together. After a few seconds, open your hands and, miraculously, the one dollar has turned into two.

Here's how: Before starting the trick, place a folded dollar bill in your collar (fig. 1). It should be sticking out just a little. Then start rubbing the borrowed dollar on your left elbow (fig. 2). As the audience is watching you rub, you will easily be able to snatch the hidden dollar from your collar (fig. 3). Quickly bring your hands together and start to rub (fig. 4). Then open your hands and show that you've magically turned one dollar into two (fig. 5).

FIGURE 1   **FIGURE 2**   **FIGURE 3**   **FIGURE 4**   **FIGURE 5**

VANISHING DOLLAR

Here is another trick where you use your "magic elbow" to achieve a great effect—only this time, instead of doubling your dollar, you will make it disappear completely. Start by borrowing a dollar bill and folding it in half, then in half again (fig. 1). Press it against your elbow and begin to rub (fig. 2).

After a few seconds, pretend to let the dollar slip out from your hand and fall to the floor. Act embarrassed as you bend down to pick up the dollar, claiming that sometimes the forces of magic are difficult to control. Resume rubbing the dollar on your elbow and, after a few seconds, the dollar again falls from your hand to the floor. As you apologize for the miscue, bend down to retrieve the dollar again. This time, however, instead of snatching the dollar from the ground, flick it under your shoe (fig. 3). If you position your foot near the dollar when you bend to pick it up, you should have no trouble raising your foot and scooping it under with no one seeing. To end the trick, stand up and resume rubbing your elbow—as if the dollar was still in your hand. Then slowly remove your hand to show that the dollar has disappeared (fig. 4).

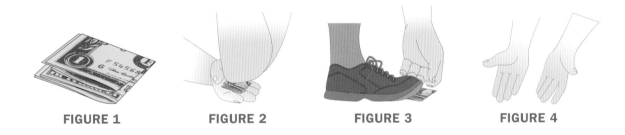

FIGURE 1   **FIGURE 2**   **FIGURE 3**   **FIGURE 4**

E$P

Feats of mentalism are among the most baffling and entertaining forms of magic ever created. You can always count on a tremendous response when demonstrating your ESP skills. In this chapter, I present several top-notch mind-reading tricks that will leave your audience astounded. By using the serial numbers on dollar bills, you will be able to "prove" that you have the ability to read minds and predict the future. The look on spectators' faces when they see you steal the thoughts out of their very brains will be priceless. The next several tricks will provide the inside secrets you need to display your psychic talents. Once you get the basics, you can personalize the tricks by building your own stories around them. Feel free to enlist your audience to help you "summon the psychic spirits" by chanting something outrageous or doing a mystical swami dance. The greater the buildup, the more spectacular the conclusion will be. So get out your crystal ball and uncover the secrets of mind reading . . .

MYSTICAL MONEY

Ready to show off your ESP skills? Ask a spectator to take several one dollar bills from his wallet and stack them neatly on a table faceup (fig. 1). If he does not have enough bills, you can provide him with a stack—just ask him to mix up the order before placing them on the table. The order of the bills must appear to be random.

Place a sealed envelope on top of the stack (fig. 2). Inside the envelope is an index card with a number written on it. The payoff comes when you ask the spectator to open the envelope and pull out the index card. Imagine his shock when he sees that the number on the index card matches the serial number of the top dollar in the stack!

Solution: Before your performance, select a dollar bill and write the serial number on an index card. Seal the index card in an envelope and you're ready to begin. Hide the dollar bill that matches the serial number under the envelope (fig. 3). So when you place the envelope on the stack, the hidden dollar will be the top bill (fig. 4).

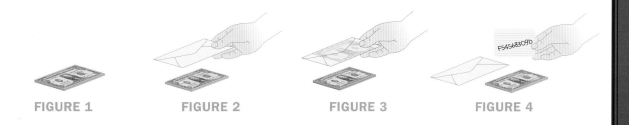

FIGURE 1   **FIGURE 2**   **FIGURE 3**   **FIGURE 4**

IT ALL ADDS UP

This top-notch dollar bill trick will prove to spectators that you have the ability to read minds. Follow the steps closely, and you will learn one of the most spectacular psychic stunts ever invented. Start with the following items: A dollar bill (of course), an envelope, a sheet of paper, and a pencil. (fig. 1). Write the numbers 1, 2, and 3 on the piece of paper and put it on a table (fig. 2). Begin the trick by handing a spectator a sealed envelope. This always adds a touch of intrigue.

Next, ask a spectator to come up to the table and write a three-digit number on the piece of paper. Ask two more spectators to come up and write three-digit numbers on the paper (one at a time). At this point, there will be 3 three-digit numbers on the page. Finally, you ask another spectator to come up, add the numbers, and announce the total. This total will be a four-digit number (fig. 3).

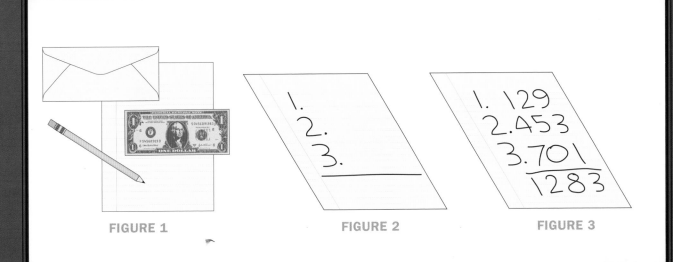

FIGURE 1

FIGURE 2

FIGURE 3

Remember that spectator who has the envelope? Well, it's time to bring her up to present the conclusion. Ask her to open the envelope and remove its contents. When she opens it, she will find a one dollar bill inside (fig. 4). Then ask her to read the last four digits of the serial number out loud (fig. 5). And, surprise, surprise! The last four digits of the serial number match the four-digit total that was on the paper!

"How?" you ask. The answer lies in the piece of paper. Before you start the trick, you will have 3 three-digit numbers already written on the other side of the paper (fig. 6). These numbers will add up to a four-digit number. And, of course, this four-digit number will match the last four numbers in the serial number of the dollar bill you had preselected. So when you ask the last spectator to come up to the table and add up the numbers, make sure you are holding the sheet of paper in your hand. When you put the paper back on the table, simply place it down with your preset numbers facing up. Works every time!

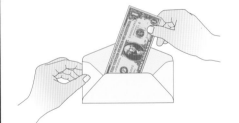

FIGURE 4

1. 129
2. 453
3. 701

1283

FIGURE 5

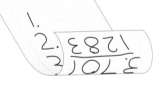

FIGURE 6

IT ALL ADDS UP — PART II

A calculator, an envelope, a dollar bill, and a few spectators are all you need to demonstrate your amazing psychic powers. Similar to the preceding trick, you will begin by sealing a dollar bill in an envelope. Hand the sealed envelope to a spectator for safekeeping. Then pull out a calculator and ask someone to enter a seven-digit number. Once that is done, take the calculator, hit the Add key and ask a second spectator to enter a seven-digit number. You then hit the Add key once again and ask a third spectator to enter a seven-digit number (fig. 1).

Finally, you announce that you will total the numbers. Hit one key on the calculator and hand it to a spectator. There will be an eight-digit number on the calculator screen. Ask the person holding the envelope to open it and remove its contents. When she pulls out the dollar bill, ask her to read off the serial number. What a coincidence! The serial number matches the number on the calculator exactly.

The secret? Before starting the trick, you will enter the serial number into the calculator, hit the Memory key, and then clear the number from the screen. At the end of the trick, instead of hitting the Equal key, you will press the Memory Recall (MR) key (fig. 2). If possible, hit the key twice, so that the M disappears from the face of the calculator.

FIGURE 1

FIGURE 2

41

ONE AHEAD

A book on magic tricks would not be complete without an example of the One Ahead technique. In this trick, you will demonstrate your psychic powers as you predict the serial numbers on three dollar bills.

To begin, ask a spectator to take three single dollar bills out of his pocket and roll them into three small balls (fig. 1). Take one of the rolled-up dollar bills, hold it against your forehead (fig. 2), and predict the last four digits of the serial number. Your spectator writes your prediction on a piece of paper. Then pick up the second rolled-up dollar bill, hold it to your forehead, and predict the last four digits of that bill. The spectator writes this number down on the piece of paper. Finally, you take the last rolled-up dollar bill, hold it to your forehead, and announce your prediction. The spectator writes this number down as well (fig. 3).

The spectator then looks at the dollar bills and sees that the last four digits of each bill match your predictions perfectly. "But how is this possible?" you ask. It's the One Ahead principle, one of the greatest mind-reading methods ever invented. By knowing the answer to *one* of the serial numbers, you will be able to predict *all* the serial numbers. Let's take a closer look . . .

FIGURE 1

FIGURE 2

3094
8736
5126

FIGURE 3

At the beginning of the trick you will take a dollar bill, memorize the last four digits of the serial number (fig. 4), and then roll it up into a ball. Keep this bill hidden in your hand, just underneath your pinky and ring finger (fig. 5).

As mentioned earlier, you then start the trick by asking your spectator to take out three dollar bills from his pocket. Watch closely as he rolls up the first dollar bill. When he puts it on the table, walk over and say, "No, make it a *tight* ball." You then pick up the rolled-up bill, take it in your hand, and twist it very tightly against the palm of your other hand to demonstrate (fig. 6). Then, instead of putting that dollar back on the table, switch it with the one that you had hidden in your hand (fig. 7). At some point, you will need to get rid of the extra dollar you switched.

When he has finished rolling all three bills, you reach for one of them and hold it to your forehead. Make sure that you do not pick the bill you planted! After pretending to concentrate, you will then predict the last four numbers of the serial number.

How will you know the number when you can't see it? You won't—but that doesn't matter. Just say the four digits that you had memorized earlier. Tell your spectator to write this prediction on a piece of paper.

FIGURE 4

FIGURE 5

FIGURE 6

FIGURE 7

You then unroll the dollar bill and look at the serial number. Pretend that you are checking to verify your prediction; but what you are really doing is sneaking a peak at the last four digits in the serial number (fig. 8). Why? Because *this is the number you will use for your next prediction!* You then reach for the next rolled-up dollar—again, do not select the bill you switched at the beginning (save that one for last). Hold the second dollar to your head, concentrate, and state your prediction. This will be easy—all you have to do is recite the digits you just memorized on the preceding dollar bill. Your spectator will then write down your second prediction. Then unroll the second bill (pretending to verify your prediction) and memorize the last four digits. This is so that you'll know what to predict for the *next* serial number.

Finally, pick up the last rolled up dollar bill (the one you switched at the beginning) and go through the same mind-reading routine. Your prediction will be the number you just saw on the preceding dollar bill. Your spectator will write down this number as well. So now the piece of paper will show your three predictions. Simply hand over the bills (mixing up the order as you do) and your spectator will see that your predictions do indeed match the serial numbers.

FIGURE 8

NUMBERS

Numbers is an amazing psychic demonstration that you would perform with a trusted partner. While your partner leaves the room, borrow a dollar bill from a spectator. Write the eight-digit serial number on an index card and return the bill to the spectator. Read the serial number from your index card aloud so the spectator can verify its authenticity. When your partner returns to the room, she is able to correctly recite the serial number.

Here's how: It is a simple code that you have with your partner. Each number corresponds with a letter of the alphabet: A = 1, B = 2, C = 3, D = 4, E = 5, F = 6, G = 7, H = 8, I = 9, J = 0.

You will give your partner clues disguised as encouragement. You can say the clues to either your partner or to the audience. Each clue will start with the appropriate letter. For example, let's say the serial number is 32475409. First, break the number down into two groups of four to make things simpler: 3247 and 5409. Start by saying: **C**oncentrate! **B**e very quiet. **D**on't make a sound. **G**ive her some time. Do you see how the first letter of each clue corresponds to the appropriate number? C, B, D, G = 3247. Continue the code with the last four numbers. Your partner will announce the serial number in two groups of four to make it easier to remember. Check below for hints for each letter.

1 (A)	2 (B)	3 (C)	4 (D)	5 (E)
Alright, concentrate	**Be quiet!**	**Concentrate!**	**Don't make a sound**	**Everyone focus**
Are you ready?	**Better not move**	**Careful!**	**Deep in thought**	**Enough talking!**

6 (F)	7 (G)	8 (H)	9 (I)	0 (J)
Focus!	**Give her some time**	**Here she goes**	**I'm sure she's getting it**	**Just relax**
Feel the vibes	**Go for it!**	**Have you got it?**	**I need silence**	**Just about there**

MATH MAGIC

Ask your friend to take a dollar out of his pocket, making sure that you don't see it. Then have him follow these steps:

1. **Add up the numbers in the serial number.**
2. **Multiply the total by 9.**
3. **Add the numbers in the product.**
4. **If it's a single digit, he's done. If it's more than a single digit, add those numbers together.**

When he says he has performed all the steps, all you have to do is reveal the final number to him. "How?" you ask. Easy! If he follows the instructions you gave him, the final number will always be 9. (See below for an example.)

When you reveal the number, use some creativity. Either have the answer sealed in an envelope for your friend to open . . . or simply feel the dollar with your finger tips until the answer "just comes to you." If you'd like a more spectacular finish, give your friend a phone number to call. Tell him to ask whoever answers what his number is. Miraculously, the person on the other end says 9 (of course, you will have arranged this with another friend ahead of time).

HERE'S AN EXAMPLE: LET'S SAY THAT THE SERIAL NUMBER WAS 89485767.

Step 1: Add the numbers: 8 + 9 + 4 + 8 + 5 + 7 + 6 + 7 = 54.
Step 2: Multiply the total by 9: 54 x 9 = 486
Step 3: Add the numbers in the product: 4 + 8 + 6 = 18
Step 4: It's a two-digit number, so add those numbers: 1 + 8 = 9

Hidden $ecrets

How well do you know a dollar bill? You've probably spent enough of them in your lifetime, but have you ever taken a really good look at one? If you were asked to list 10 features on a dollar bill, could you? Chances are that you know George Washington's portrait is on the front of the bill, and that there is a serial number and a date somewhere nearby. But did you know that there's an eagle and a pyramid on the back of the bill? You may also be interested to know that both sides of the Great Seal of the United States are printed on either side of the giant ONE on the back. This is where you will find the eagle holding an olive branch in his right talon and a bunch of arrows in his left. You can also see the eagle facing in the direction of the olive branch, indicating his preference for peace over war.

Now that you know some of the basics, this chapter will arm you with secrets and little known facts you can use to trick, stump, and dazzle friends and strangers. It will also show you how to fold and roll dollar bills to perform some fun and interesting tricks.

ONE ISN'T SO LONELY

Challenge your friends to answer the following question: *How many times does the number one appear on every dollar bill?* And, yes, peeking is allowed! Before looking at the solution, inspect a dollar bill and try counting them yourself.

How many did you get? Eight? Sixteen? The correct answer is actually 18. The numeral *1* appears nine times and the spelled *one* appears eight times. There's also a Roman numeral *I* that appears once. The first mistake many people make is not counting both forms of the number (1 and one). Since the serial number and series date change on every bill, they cannot be counted.

Most people will quickly find the four numeral *1*s on the front and back corners. And with a little investigation, they will soon discover the spelled *one* on each corner on the back (fig. 1), as well as the *one* on the bottom of the front and back. And the giant *ONE* on the back is generally not too difficult to locate. It is the last four that are more elusive. If you look carefully, there is a *1* on the front of the bill in the date printed on the green seal of the Department of the Treasury (fig. 2). In the same area there is the lightly printed word, *ONE*, covering the seal (fig. 2). And finally, there is a Roman numeral *I* written in small print at the bottom of the pyramid on the back (fig 1).

FIGURE 1

FIGURE 2

THE *I*s HAVE IT

Similar to the preceding challenge, this one poses the question: *How many Is are on a one dollar bill?* Again, before peeking at the answer, count them yourself and see how many you can find. Well, how did you do? Did you get all 22? This one is a lot trickier because of the ways the question can be interpreted. You probably found most or all of the *I*s, but did you also count the *eyes* on the dollar bill?

The front: The letter *I* can be found in the words United, America, this, is, public, private, Washington (D.C.), Washington (the president), Series, and United (again, bottom left). And let's not forget George Washington's two *eyes*!

The back: United, America, In, Annuit, Cœptis, and United (again). The other four are the most difficult to find. If you look closely, you will see that the eagle on the right has an *eye*. And slightly above and to the left of the eagle, you can see the word *Pluribus*. Also, there is an *eye* floating on top of the pyramid on the left. And the one that is sure to stump even the most careful observers is in the Roman numeral date at the bottom of the pyramid: MDCCLXXVI.

FIGURE 1

13

Do you think that the number 13 is unlucky? If so, then you may change your mind when you find out how important the number 13 is to the United States and the dollar bill. Representing the 13 original colonies, the number 13 is ubiquitous on the dollar. For starters, the front of the dollar bill features a green Department of the Treasury seal. Within the seal, there is a chevron with 13 stars. But it's the back of the dollar that is more interesting. Can you find the other representations of 13?

There are many of them, all located within the two halves of The Great Seal of the United States (figs. 1 and 2). If you look closely you can see 13: Stars above the eagle, arrows, leaves on the olive branch, fruits on the olive branch, bars on the shield, letters in "E Pluribus Unum," letters in "Annuit Cœptis," and brick rows on the pyramid.

FIGURE 1

FIGURE 2

HIDE & SEEK

Now that you've gotten the hang of finding 1s and Is, here are a few more challenges:

Q: HOW MANY 2s ARE ON THE FRONT OF EVERY NEW TWENTY DOLLAR BILL?
A: There are five. Don't forget that there's a 2 in every "new" dollar bill, since the new ones will all have a 2 in the date. (Not counting, of course, the microprinted 2s embedded as a security measure.)

Q: HOW MANY 10s ARE ON EVERY TEN DOLLAR BILL?
A: Twelve. The numeral 10 appears eight times, and *ten* appears four times, including the phrase, legal *ten*der, on the front left.

Q: HOW MANY HEADS ARE ON A ONE DOLLAR BILL?
A: Fifteen. One George Washington head, one eagle head, and 13 arrowheads (in the eagle's talon).

IN THE FOLD

Knowing where to fold a dollar is the secret to some interesting dollar bill quirks. For example:

How do you turn 2 one-dollar bills into a 10? Easy! Roll them up and make them look like figure 1.

If you'd like to watch your friend's eyes bulge with fear, try this: Ask to borrow a twenty dollar bill and then tear it in half. Well, at least make it look as though you're tearing it in half. First hold the bill as if you're about to tear it (fig. 2). Then bring your right hand down quickly, folding the bill over in half (fig. 3). The quick motion will sound like the bill is tearing.

Want another way to pretend to rip a dollar bill? Hold the bill as in figure 2. Then bring the bill to your mouth, purse your lips, and suddenly blow out a burst of air as your right hand moves quickly down the bill, folding it back in half (fig. 3). It sounds exactly like a dollar bill tearing.

Here's how to fold a dollar bill to show an ideal girlfriend. First, find the phrase on the front of the dollar (top left) that says, "THIS NOTE IS LEGAL TENDER FOR ALL DEBTS, PUBLIC AND PRIVATE." Fold the front left of the bill underneath, so that the words, THIS NOTE IS, are folded under (fig. 4). With your left thumb, cover the letters L and E in LEGAL, so that it now says, "GAL TENDER AND PRIVATE" (fig. 5).

FIGURE 1

FIGURE 2

FIGURE 3

FIGURE 4

FIGURE 5

TURN AROUND IS FAIR PLAY

Here is a simple and fun trick you can use with no setup or preparation. You will be able to mysteriously flip a dollar bill upside down without turning it over. Start by holding a dollar bill with both hands, George Washington facing your audience (fig. 1). Fold the dollar in half backward lengthwise (fig. 2). Then fold the left side forward over to the right (fig. 3). Fold it once more forward from left to right (fig. 4). Pause and hold the folded dollar for everyone to see. At this point, you should be looking at an upside down numeral 1 on the right (fig. 4). Unfold the dollar backward from right to left, so that you now see the numeral 1 on the left (fig. 5). Unfold the dollar once more backward to the right. Now you should see the bottom half of George Washington's face (fig. 6). All you have to do now is unfold the bill toward your audience, showing them an *upside down* George Washington (fig. 7).

FIGURE 1

FIGURE 2

FIGURE 3

FIGURE 4

FIGURE 5

FIGURE 6

FIGURE 7

ROLL OVER

Here's a magic trick that requires no magic; no sleight of hand; no secret codes. It works all by itself. Start by holding a five dollar bill with Abe Lincoln staring you in the face. Lay a one dollar bill over the five so it makes an upside down T as shown in fig. 1. Pick up the bills in that position and begin to roll them up into a cylinder (fig. 2). Continue rolling until the one dollar bill has been rolled completely (fig. 3). Then all you have to do is unroll the bills and, amazingly, the five dollar bill is now *on top* of the one dollar bill (fig. 4).

This is because once the five dollar bill has been rolled, it reverses its position as you continue to roll the one dollar bill. Practice a few times and see for yourself.

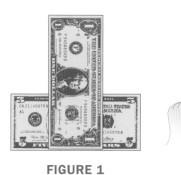

FIGURE 1

FIGURE 2

FIGURE 3

FIGURE 4

$windled!

What good is magic if you can't use it to win a few friendly bets? This chapter is dedicated to tricks, challenges, and dares with dollar bills that could very well earn you free drinks. Each trick in this chapter will bamboozle, deceive, and outrage your closest friends and acquaintances. Although none of these entries requires any special skill or practice, you do need to have a considerable amount of gall to pull them off. You see, once your friends realize they've been swindled, you may need to use some magic to make yourself disappear in a flash.

POWER OF MONEY

The effect of this trick leaves spectators baffled. Begin by asking a spectator to hold a pencil by both ends (fig. 1). Then pull a crisp one dollar bill from your pocket and ask a spectator to inspect it. Once it passes inspection as legitimate, announce that the dollar bill, combined with sheer mental power, is strong enough to break a pencil in two. Fold the dollar bill from top to bottom and hold it between your thumb and middle finger (fig. 2). Place the bill on the pencil and concentrate (fig. 3). Slowly and deliberately lift the bill and come down swiftly on the pencil, breaking it in two instantly (fig. 4).

The secret? Just before you strike the pencil with the bill, extend your index finger forward into the fold of the dollar (fig. 5). With some practice, you will find that your finger can break the pencil easily.

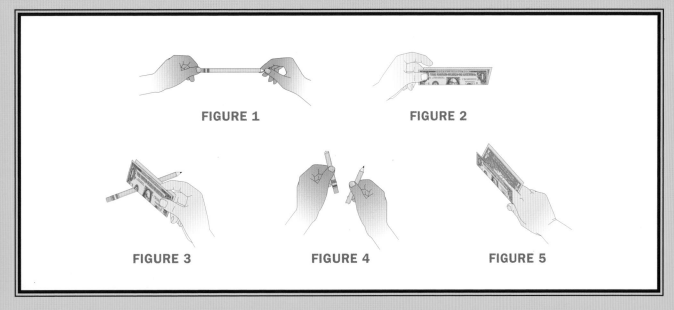

FIGURE 1

FIGURE 2

FIGURE 3

FIGURE 4

FIGURE 5

GOTCHA!

On the surface, Gotcha! appears to be a ridiculously simple trick that will surely make people groan . . . but then turns out to be a diabolical ruse that ends with you sneering at your spectators and shouting, *"Gotcha!"*

Begin by taking a one dollar bill and placing it on a table in plain sight. Then place a book or other solid object on top of the bill, covering it completely. You announce to your subjects that you will be able to remove the dollar without touching or disturbing the book in any way.

Impossible, you say? Well, so will they! Once they express their disbelief, you wave your hands over the book—or use your favorite conjuring technique—and then open your hand and show them a one dollar bill that you had hidden in your hand. You say, "See? I snatched the dollar and didn't touch the book!" Of course, your spectators will groan and accuse you of showing a different dollar. Shocked that they would doubt you, challenge them to lift the book and check to see if the dollar is still there. As soon as someone removes the book, you quickly grab the original dollar bill from the table, sneer at them, and shout, *"Gotcha!"*

FIGURE 1

FIGURE 2

FIGURE 3

FIGURE 4

TALKING DOLLAR

In front of your audience, you announce, "I have a fifty dollar bill that says I can levitate in midair for thirty seconds." Then ask if anyone would like to take you up on your bet. Of course, your spectators will see this as easy money and will fall over themselves to accept your challenge. Once the bets have been placed, get ready to collect your earnings and make a quick getaway.

Here's how: Before you begin the trick, write the following on a small sticky note and attach it to the front of a fifty dollar bill: "I can levitate in midair for thirty seconds." If you want to be cute about it, draw a talk bubble around the words coming from President Grant's mouth. Then collect your money and escape before the crowd turns ugly.

ROLLING DOLLARS

Here is a challenge that will surely leave your audience baffled. Lay a crisp dollar bill on a table face up and then place a bottle (empty, of course!) upside down on top of it (fig. 1). Then challenge your spectators to remove the dollar bill without touching the bottle or letting it fall.

Is it possible to quickly snatch the bill from under the bottle without tipping it over? Well, it is, but that will require a lot of practice and considerable skill. A much safer and more effective way is to simply roll the dollar bill out from under the bottle. Begin by taking one end of the dollar, and slowly rolling it toward the bottle (fig. 2). When the bill reaches the bottle, continue to roll and you will see the rest of the bill move toward you and pass under the bottle. Soon you will have the bill rolled tightly and completely free from the bottle (fig. 3).

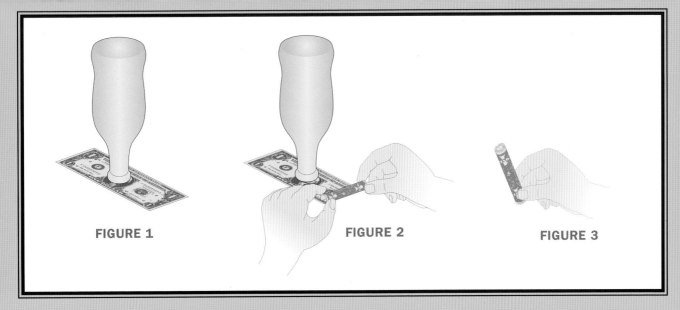

FIGURE 1

FIGURE 2

FIGURE 3

SNATCH!

If you've been seeking a sure-fire way to win a bet, look no further. Snatch! is the perfect trick. Hold a dollar bill between the thumb and index finger of your left hand, as indicated in figure 1. Let the bill fall and snatch it with your right hand as in figure 2. Do this several times, demonstrating to your spectators how easy it is.

Ask them, "See how simple it is to snatch the dollar?" Once they agree, challenge one of them to try to snatch the dollar when you let it fall. Chances are, your friend would be willing to bet large sums of money that he can snatch the dollar. But you're not the type of person who would take advantage of his friends like that . . . or are you?

When your spectator is ready to try, hold the bill with your left hand as seen in figure 1. Ask him to place his thumb and index finger around the center of the bill—not touching it, but very close (fig. 3).

You can mention that since his fingers are so close, he should have no problem snatching the dollar as it falls. But the joke will be on him, because no matter how many times he tries, he will never be able to snatch the dollar (fig. 4). Try it again and again; he will never succeed. Just make sure he doesn't cheat by anticipating the drop.

FIGURE 1

FIGURE 2

FIGURE 3

FIGURE 4

Trick Index